ALGORITHMIC GOLD:

The New Billionaires Of X Social Media

ONESIMUS MALATJI

ALGORITHMIC GOLD: The New Billionaires Of X Social Media

By: Onesimus Malatji

DEDICATION

Being one of the difficulties in my family, always stubborn, I thank God I turned out alright. I dedicate this book to my mother, Esther Malatji. I will always love you. You have raised me well until I became a fully grown man. Thank you for your prayers and support during my tough times in life. Additionally, I extend my heartfelt dedication to my beautiful wife, the partner of my life, Petunia. You have been there for me and our family, and you are truly one in a million – the best motivator. I thank God for having you as my spouse, partner, and my inspiration; you are one of my most special and wonderful gifts. During times of trials, you have never walked out on us. Thank you. I love you so much.

I also send this dedication to my brother Edward "Gong," one of the greatest creative businesspersons alive. Thank you for being a wonderful brother and supporting me in times of need and trial. May God bless you and increase your business anointing. I love you so much. Special greetings to my sister Bertha, your passion for food will undoubtedly touch the world. I love you.

Furthermore, I extend my love and dedication to my brother Mohau; I will always cherish you, brother. Special Dedication for Galetsang & Dineo I will always love you no matter what. This is also for my friends, and fellow soldiers in war: Zama, Panana, Fina, Tshwane, Blessing, Lowen, Neo, Kiki**(Sponge Bob)** I love you guys – you are my family. Special Gratitude to my inspirer my mother. I deeply respect the gift that God has put in you, and I am immensely grateful for having you while I was putting this book together.

Thank you, my dear mother, Esther Malatji. I love you so much

ACKNOWLEDGMENTS

I extend my deepest gratitude to everyone who has been a part of this incredible journey, both seen and unseen. Your support, encouragement, and unwavering belief in me have been the driving force behind the creation of this book.

To my family, for standing by me through thick and thin, for believing in my dreams, and for being a constant source of inspiration – your love and encouragement have been my guiding light.

To my friends, mentors, and colleagues, your valuable insights and feedback have shaped the ideas within these pages. Your willingness to share your wisdom and experiences has enriched this work beyond measure.

To all those who have supported me on my path, whether through a kind word, a helping hand, or a moment of shared understanding, thank you. Your presence in my life has made all the difference.

To the countless individuals who have faced challenges and setbacks, yet continued to strive for greatness, your stories have fueled the inspiration behind these words. May you find solace and encouragement within these pages.

And finally, to the readers who have embarked on this journey with me, thank you for allowing me to share my thoughts and experiences. It is my hope that this book serves as a beacon of hope, a source of guidance, and a reminder that fulfillment can be found in every step of life's intricate tapestry.

With heartfelt appreciation,

Onesimus Malatji

ALGORITHMIC GOLD:

The New Billionaires Of X Social Media

TABLE OF CONTECT   PAGES

ALGORITHMIC GOLD:

The New Billionaires Of X Social Media

INTRODUCTION: SETTING THE STAGE - THE NEW DIGITAL ERA

Welcome to the threshold of the new digital frontier, an era where traditional paradigms of business, social engagement, and personal branding are not just being challenged—they are being upended entirely. This is not merely an age of change but an age of unprecedented revolutions. And right at the heart of these revolutions is X Social Media, a platform that has transformed from a simple microblogging site into an intricate web of opportunities, a gold mine of untapped potentials.

Imagine a world where every post, every interaction, and every impression on your social media account can be turned into financial gains. Think beyond the traditional confines of advertising revenue and paid sponsorships. What if your social media presence alone could become a significant revenue stream, and in turn, catapult you into the realm of digital billionaires? This is no longer the stuff of science fiction. With X Social Media's radical new algorithms and monetization strategies, this fantasy is now a reality.

But the digital ecosystem is far broader than X alone. The tidal wave of innovation extends to cryptocurrencies, with alternatives like Ethereum, XRP, and Dogecoin promising not just investment avenues but also entirely new ways to transact and engage online. Add to that the increasing influence of artificial intelligence, which promises to overhaul traditional work streams, empower creators, and even pioneer new career paths, and you have a landscape ripe for exploration and exploitation.

This book, "Algorithmic Gold: The New Billionaires of X Social Media," aims to be your definitive guide through these thrilling yet complex landscapes. It brings together a blend of in-depth analysis, case studies, actionable strategies, and a look at what the future holds, offering you a comprehensive toolkit to navigate this brave new digital world.

Whether you are a digital marketer, a content creator, a tech enthusiast, or someone merely interested in understanding the seismic shifts happening in our digital lives, this book will equip you with the necessary knowledge and insights to stake your claim in the future. You'll learn not just how to survive but thrive in this new era—maximizing profits, optimizing engagement, and turning algorithmic sequences into your personal goldmine.

So, are you ready to dig for your share of Algorithmic Gold? Let's dive in.

THE REBRANDING OF TWITTER TO X - A NEW DAWN REIMAGINED

In the annals of digital history, few moments have been as pivotal as the day when Twitter—once a simple platform for 280-character thoughts—was bought and rebranded by Elon Musk to become X social media. The platform, already a significant player in the social media landscape, metamorphosed into an intricate, multi-layered ecosystem that blurred the lines between social networking, business, and personal branding. It signalled a new dawn not just for the platform itself, but for the broader digital universe.

A New Ownership, A New Vision

Elon Musk, a name synonymous with paradigm-shifting ventures like Tesla and SpaceX, brought his Midas touch to the social media realm. His acquisition of Twitter was more than just a business transaction; it was a complete reimagination of what social media could achieve. Musk envisioned a platform free from the menace of bots, a space that encourages meaningful interactions while rewarding its users. A monthly subscription model was introduced as an anti-bot measure, making it cost-prohibitive for automated accounts to flood the platform, thereby significantly enhancing user experience.

Why "X"?

The name "X" serves more than just branding aesthetics. It represents the 'X-factor,' the unknown variable that can have a profound impact on an equation. In the case of X Social Media, this variable is you—the user. The platform has democratized the concept of value creation, making each user a potential revenue generator, a small-scale entrepreneur, or even a digital billionaire. X isn't just a playground for celebrities; it's an arena for anyone willing to invest in their digital presence.

A Shift in Monetization: The Algorithmic Gold

Under the new management, X introduced an algorithmic-based revenue model that promised to pay users based on the 'impressions' their posts generated. Gone are the days when advertisers were the only stakeholders who profited from your data and engagement. Now, each post, each impression, each interaction counts—literally. Users could, for the first time, earn directly from their content, based on how many people it reached and engaged with, providing a strong monetary incentive for creativity and quality content.

The Power of the Blue Tick

In a genius move, X tweaked the dynamics around the much-coveted blue tick. Now, the verification badge wasn't just an elitist symbol but a gateway to greater revenue. For those with a significant following, the blue tick came as a given, but for the rest, achieving a certain threshold of impressions was the golden ticket. This democratization of the blue tick not only motivated users to create high-quality content but also made the platform more inclusive.

The Landscape of Shadow Banning

The innovative features came with their share of pitfalls. Users now had to be extra cautious about their activities to avoid 'shadow banning,' a practice that could significantly decrease their impressions and, by extension, their revenue. X made it clear—while the potential for earnings was massive, users had to play by the rules.

As we turn the page on this new chapter in social media history, X has not just redefined the rules of the game; it has changed the game entirely. Through this book, you will explore these changes in-depth and learn how to navigate the waves of opportunities and challenges they bring. As Musk's X has shown, we're not just passive consumers of content anymore; we are active participants in a digital ecosystem that promises 'Algorithmic Gold.'

Are you ready to explore this goldmine? Onward we go.

ALGORITHMIC GOLD: UNDERSTANDING X'S REVENUE MODEL

In the first chapter, we glimpsed at how the rebranding of Twitter to X social media has ushered in a new era for social platforms, content creators, and consumers alike. This ground-breaking shift is deeply rooted in X's unique revenue model, a sophisticated system that doesn't just provide value to advertisers or the platform itself, but extends the opportunity for financial gains to each and every user.

Breaking Down the Revenue Model

X's revenue model is based on a combination of traditional advertising, subscription fees, and an innovative algorithm that calculates and pays out user earnings based on "impressions." While the exact formula behind the algorithm remains a closely guarded secret, it's evident that the more engagement your content generates—in the form of likes, retweets, and comments—the more impressions it garners, and the more you earn.

The Power of Impressions

In the world of X, impressions aren't just metrics; they are a form of currency. Every post, every interaction contributes to your earnings, thereby making quality and creativity the prime drivers of financial success. It encourages users to go beyond mere self-expression, urging them to create content that resonates with a wider audience. For businesses and marketers, this model offers a transparent and equitable way to calculate ROI, thus breaking away from the nebulous metrics of old.

The Premium Tier: Unlocking Additional Benefits

While X's basic functionalities remain free, subscribing to the Premium tier opens up a treasure trove of additional features. Not only does it allow you to escape the shackles of 280 characters, but it also unlocks text formatting, fewer ads, and an all-important "edit" button. But the most significant feature is the prioritization in rankings, both in conversations and in search results. Premium users are given an algorithmic leg-up, ensuring their content has a higher chance of being seen—and hence, earning more.

Monetizing Videos and Long-form Content

The introduction of video monetization is another game-changer. Unlike its predecessor, X allows users to earn impressions from video content, expanding the avenues for content creation and monetization. Whether you are a vlogger, an educator, or a visual artist, the video feature enables you to diversify your content while growing your earnings.

Understanding the "Shadow Ban"

As enticing as the revenue model may seem, it comes with its caveats. X's algorithm is designed to detect and "shadow ban" users who violate the platform's guidelines or engage in spammy behavior. A shadow ban significantly reduces a user's visibility on the platform, which in turn severely impacts their impressions and earnings. It serves as a regulatory mechanism, ensuring that users adhere to ethical and qualitative standards.

Play the Long Game

Given the revenue potential, the temptation to game the system is high. But X is built for sustainability, rewarding those who play the long game. Consistency, authenticity, and quality are the cornerstones of success on this platform.

In the chapters to come, we'll delve deeper into how you can maximize your earnings, expand your digital portfolio, and even explore synergies between X and other emerging technologies like cryptocurrency and AI. The digital gold rush has just begun, and X Social Media is where you stake your claim.

Are you ready to dig deeper into this algorithmic goldmine? Let's unearth the treasures that await.

X'S ANTI-BOT STRATEGY: THE RISE OF THE SUBSCRIPTION MODEL

X social media, in its quest to redefine the digital landscape, faced an obstacle that many other platforms have wrestled with: the proliferation of bots. These automated accounts have been employed for various purposes, ranging from harmless automations to insidious activities like spamming, disseminating fake news, and even attempting to manipulate public opinion. Elon Musk, the visionary behind X's transformation, described it as a "super tough problem." His solution? A radical shift towards a subscription model.

The Necessity of a Subscription Model

While a subscription model isn't novel in the digital realm, the way X has implemented it is ground-breaking. It serves multiple purposes— enhanced features for subscribers, a new revenue stream for the platform, and a robust barrier against bots. By putting a price on account creation, X has elevated the cost of running bots to an unsustainable level for most spammers and manipulators.

Premium: More Than Just An Edit Button

At face value, X's Premium subscription appears to offer perks like an edit button, prioritized rankings, and extended character limits for tweets. But what it also does is act as a filtration mechanism. Those who opt for the subscription are often serious content creators, marketers, or individuals who see value in the platform's unique offerings, separating them from casual or malicious users.

Combating the "Vast Armies of Bots"

Under the new subscription model, every new account has to be tied to a unique payment method, making it cumbersome and expensive to create bots end masse. It's not fool proof, but it significantly raises the bar for those seeking to misuse the platform. By making bot creation cost-prohibitive, X effectively minimizes their impact, enhancing the overall user experience and ensuring more equitable distribution of impressions and earnings.

Payment Method as a Security Layer

The mandatory payment method adds an additional layer of verification to user accounts, creating a rudimentary but effective trust system. While not without its privacy concerns, this method serves to associate each account with a real individual or entity, thereby contributing to the platform's credibility and the veracity of its content.

The Impact on User Experience

By curbing the number of bots, X has enhanced the authenticity of interactions on its platform. Users can now engage more freely, knowing that their impressions are more likely to come from real people and that their content is less likely to be drowned out by automated spam or manipulation.

Balancing Inclusion and Exclusivity

One critique of the subscription model is that it risks making the platform less inclusive. However, X has striven to maintain a balance. Basic functionalities remain free, and the monetary barrier for account creation primarily targets the bot issue, not genuine users who can't afford the subscription.

In conclusion, X's transition to a subscription model isn't just a revenue-generating tactic; it's a comprehensive strategy to enrich user interaction, combat bots, and elevate the platform's overall quality. The true ingenuity lies in how these various goals are achieved simultaneously, a feat that sets X social media apart in the digital universe.

In the next chapter, we will delve into how X seamlessly integrates with emerging technologies like cryptocurrencies and AI, enhancing not only its own ecosystem but also opening new frontiers in the digital world. Stay tuned.

THE BLUE TICK PARADIGM

In the world of social media, the verified blue tick has long been a symbol of status and credibility. On X social media, however, the blue tick serves not just as an emblem of prestige, but as a gateway to financial prosperity and community influence. The rebranded platform has reimagined the concept of verification, tying it into its broader monetization and anti-bot strategy.

The Blue Tick as an Earnings Multiplier

In the days of Twitter, the blue tick largely served as a symbol of identity verification for public figures, celebrities, and brands. But on X, the coveted blue tick also grants its bearers access to higher revenue streams, thanks to a multi-tiered algorithmic revenue model. While anyone with a subscription can earn through impressions, verified accounts get a revenue boost, incentivizing more quality content and genuine engagement.

Earning Your Blue Tick: The New Metrics

Gone are the days where verification was the exclusive domain of the well-known and well-connected. On X, the blue tick can be earned by anyone who demonstrates high engagement over a specified period. For example, users who generate 5 million impressions over the last three months have the opportunity to join the blue tick club, levelling the playing field for hardworking, creative individuals.

Blue Tick Benefits: More Than Just Prestige

Beyond revenue multipliers and algorithmic favour, the blue tick comes with its own set of perks. These include higher priority in conversation threads, advanced analytics, and access to exclusive community features. X's approach encourages a meritocracy where users are rewarded for their quality contributions to the platform.

The Role of the Blue Tick in Anti-Bot Measures

The rigorous requirements for blue tick verification also serve as a robust anti-bot measure. Given that bots are unlikely to generate meaningful, consistent engagement over time, the criteria for blue tick verification become yet another hurdle for automated accounts, further enhancing platform integrity.

Social and Economic Implications

The redefined blue tick paradigm is not just a feature but a social and economic instrument. It enables a new class of digital influencers, entrepreneurs, and creatives who can monetize their online presence effectively. It also fosters a sense of community where quality content is rewarded, and genuine interaction is encouraged.

Criticisms and Controversies

Not everyone is pleased with the monetization of the blue tick. Critics argue that it could exacerbate inequality on the platform, favouring those who can afford subscriptions and thereby creating a two-tiered system. While this critique is valid, proponents argue that X's model at least provides an attainable pathway to verification, as opposed to the opaque and often arbitrary systems of the past.

In sum, the blue tick on X social media has evolved into a multifaceted feature that serves multiple strategic purposes—from user incentivization to platform security. Its transformation exemplifies X's innovative approach to reimagining the functionalities and utilities of a social media platform.

In the next chapter, we will explore how X is leveraging video content to capture even more of the digital landscape. Keep reading to find out more.

THE PREMIUM EXPERIENCE: WHAT SUBSCRIPTIONS UNLOCK

The advent of subscription models in social media isn't new, but the way X has integrated it into its platform has set a new standard. The introduction of the Premium subscription—emerging from the foundations of Twitter Blue—opens up a whole new world of features, opportunities, and, more importantly, earning potentials for its users. Let's delve into what subscribing to X's Premium service unlocks for you.

Longer Tweets, More Expressions

With the Premium subscription, you're no longer confined to 280 characters. You can now express yourself in up to 4,000 characters per tweet, bringing a near-blogging experience to the platform. Although these extended tweets appear as a 280-character preview on timelines, a "Show more" prompt allows followers to read your entire message. This feature caters to writers, educators, activists, and anyone who wants to communicate in-depth content without resorting to long and sometimes confusing tweet threads.

The Edit Button

One of the most anticipated features of all time, the edit button, is now a reality but exclusively for Premium subscribers. Make a typo? Want to clarify a statement? With Premium, you can edit your tweets after publishing, reducing the spread of misinformation and enhancing the quality of discourse on the platform.

Prioritized Rankings

Another enticing feature of the Premium experience is prioritized ranking in conversations and search results. This feature helps to elevate the visibility of your content, thereby increasing your impressions, reach, and potential earnings. For influencers, activists, and businesses, this feature could be a game-changer.

Text Formatting and Fewer Ads

The ability to use text formatting like bold, italics, and underlining adds nuance and emphasis to your messages, allowing for richer communication. In addition, Premium subscribers enjoy an almost ad-free experience, making for a more streamlined and enjoyable user experience.

Anti-Bot Measures

By requiring a subscription fee, X aims to drastically reduce the number of bots on the platform. For Premium subscribers, this means a cleaner, more human interaction and a reduced risk of falling into misinformation traps.

The Monetization Multiplier

As discussed in earlier chapters, a Premium subscription enhances your earning capacity through the platform's algorithmic revenue model. The more you invest in Premium, the more the platform invests in you, making it a win-win for serious users and the platform itself.

Exclusive Community Features

Last but not least, Premium subscribers have access to exclusive community features, like special interest groups, advanced analytics, and more. These features help you to network with like-minded individuals more effectively, potentially opening doors to collaborations and partnerships.

The Critique: Is Premium Creating a Digital Divide?

While the Premium subscription comes with undeniable perks, it has also sparked debates over whether it's creating a digital divide between the haves and have-nots. Critics worry that these exclusive features could marginalize users who can't afford the subscription, further exacerbating social inequalities.

In conclusion, the Premium subscription on X is designed to be more than just an 'add-on.' It's an integral part of the platform's ecosystem, aimed at enhancing user experience and revenue generation. Whether or not one subscribes could significantly impact their success and influence on this revolutionary platform.

VIDEO MONETIZATION: THE UNTAPPED FRONTIER

The revolution in digital media consumption is not solely restricted to text or images; video content has surged in popularity, becoming a dominant force on various social media platforms. X is no exception. By introducing video monetization options, X has unleashed a powerful, untapped frontier for content creators and marketers alike. But how does it work, and more importantly, how can you tap into this lucrative stream? Let's explore.

Video Length and Quality: The New Norms

In contrast to its predecessor, X allows users to upload longer and higher-quality videos. This isn't just an aesthetic upgrade; it's a tactical move to attract filmmakers, vloggers, and educators to the platform. The days of grainy, truncated clips are long gone; X aims to be a space where meaningful, quality video content thrives.

Impression-Based Monetization

Similar to its text-based content, X employs an algorithmic model for video monetization that is based on impressions. However, video impressions are calculated somewhat differently, factoring in metrics like watch time, engagement, and shares. The intricacies of the algorithm might be kept under wraps, but one thing is clear: the more compelling and engaging your video, the more you stand to earn.

Subscription Leverage

If you're a Premium subscriber, your video content benefits from prioritized rankings, increasing its visibility and consequently its monetization potential. With millions of videos uploaded daily, this edge can significantly impact your earnings and outreach.

Ad Integrations

One of the most direct ways of monetizing video content is through in-video ads. While the platform has reduced the prevalence of ads for Premium users, non-subscribed users will still encounter them, providing another income stream for video creators. How the revenue is shared between creators and the platform remains a closely guarded secret, but insiders suggest it's more generous than most other platforms.

Partner Programs and Sponsored Content

Another route to monetization is through partner programs and sponsored content. While this is not exclusive to X, the platform's high engagement rates and specialized algorithms make it more lucrative for such collaborations. Brands are increasingly interested in partnering with X content creators for video campaigns, further enriching the ecosystem.

Live Streaming: The Next Big Thing

Speculations are rife about X introducing a live streaming feature, capitalizing on real-time audience engagement and potentially adding another layer to the monetization puzzle. If these rumours hold, X could soon become a one-stop-shop for all types of content creators.

Ethical Concerns: Fair Use and Copyright

As with any form of content, video monetization comes with its share of ethical concerns, particularly around copyright and fair use. X has implemented stringent guidelines and employs AI-powered tools to scan for copyrighted material. While these mechanisms aren't fool proof, they represent a step in the right direction for protecting intellectual property.

Conclusion

Video content is not merely an addition to X; it's a ground-breaking expansion that has redefined what the platform is capable of. Whether you're a novice or a seasoned content creator, understanding and leveraging video monetization on X can significantly augment your digital portfolio and earning potential.

THE GAME OF THE RABBIT HOLE

In the digital terrain of X, the "Rabbit Hole" is more than just a metaphor. It's an intricate, algorithmic journey that users embark upon, sometimes consciously but often inadvertently, as they interact with the platform. Understanding the rules of this game is vital for anyone aiming to maximize their reach and revenue. This chapter delves into how the Rabbit Hole works on X and offers strategies to navigate it successfully.

Defining the Rabbit Hole

In its simplest form, the Rabbit Hole represents a chain of content and interactions that keep users engrossed within the X ecosystem. It starts with a single click on a tweet, reply, or video, which then leads to another, and another, thus prolonging engagement and boosting impressions for creators.

Algorithmic Drivers

X's algorithm plays the role of the gatekeeper to the Rabbit Hole. It decides what content appears on your feed, which replies gain prominence, and which videos are suggested next. While the exact workings of the algorithm are proprietary, it's understood that metrics like impressions, engagement rates, and the relevance of the content play pivotal roles.

The Impact of Impressions

X's revenue model is significantly tied to impressions. The deeper a user goes down the Rabbit Hole, the more impressions are generated for various pieces of content. For creators, this means that strategically placing your content to be a part of this chain can yield substantial monetary rewards.

Shadow Banning and Its Pitfalls

One term you'll hear often among X users is "shadow banning," a phenomenon where a user's content is suppressed without any formal notice. This is the quicksand in the Rabbit Hole game; falling into it could significantly reduce your impressions and earnings. It usually happens due to violations of X's community guidelines. Learning how to avoid shadow bans is crucial for maintaining a healthy presence on the platform.

Collaboration and Network Effects

Success in the Rabbit Hole game often involves collaborative efforts. Retweets, mentions, and intelligent replies can pull audiences from one creator's content to another's. This network effect amplifies impressions and therefore revenue for all involved parties, creating a win-win scenario.

Trending Topics: Double-Edged Sword

Engaging with trending topics can rapidly boost your impressions, pushing you further down the Rabbit Hole. However, this can be a double-edged sword; trending topics often come with heightened scrutiny, both from the algorithm and the community. A single misguided tweet could result in a backlash, leading to shadow banning or even outright suspension.

Exit Strategies: Know When to Log Off

Continuous engagement with the platform is tempting but could lead to digital burnout. Knowing when to step back, take stock of your strategies, and recharge is essential. After all, the Rabbit Hole will always be there; understanding how to navigate it efficiently can make your journey both profitable and sustainable.

Conclusion

The Rabbit Hole is a fascinating aspect of X's algorithmic landscape, offering both risks and rewards. By understanding its mechanisms and pitfalls, users and creators can significantly impact their digital footprint and earnings. In the next chapter, we will explore how cryptocurrencies integrate with X's revenue model, adding yet another layer to this complex ecosystem.

THE SHADOW BAN: NAVIGATING X'S DARK SIDE

As captivating as the digital realm of X can be, it also has its pitfalls. One of the most talked-about yet least understood phenomena is the concept of shadow banning. This chapter aims to pull back the veil on this practice, exploring what it is, how it happens, and, most importantly, how to navigate around it to maintain a thriving presence on X.

What is Shadow Banning?

Shadow banning is a form of content suppression where a user's posts are not openly removed or flagged but are instead made less visible to the broader community. To the user, it appears as though everything is functioning normally, but the reach of their content is severely restricted.

How Does It Happen?

The specifics of shadow banning remain a proprietary secret, but common triggers may include repetitive content, violations of community guidelines, or algorithmic indicators that suggest spam or harmful activity. It can also happen due to mass reporting or blockings by other users, indicating to the algorithm that your content might be problematic.

Recognizing the Signs

A sudden, inexplicable drop-in engagement rates, replies, or retweets can be an indicator of a shadow ban. If your content isn't showing up in searches or hashtag streams, you might be experiencing this form of suppression.

How to Avoid Being Shadow Banned

Stay Informed: Always keep yourself updated on X's terms of service and community guidelines.

Diversify Content: Avoid repetitive posting or aggressive tagging, as these are red flags for spam-like behavior.

Engage Responsibly: Provocative or offensive material can quickly get you reported and, subsequently, shadow banned.

Audit Your Network: Being connected to other accounts that are shadow banned can decrease your account's reputation as well.

Recovering From a Shadow Ban

Self-Audit: Before appealing a shadow ban, review your recent activities to identify any potential violations you may have committed.

Contact Support: X does have an appeal process, but it can be time-consuming and offers no guarantees.

Strategize: Use the time to recalibrate your approach, refining your content strategy for when your account returns to normal.

Transparency and Advocacy

There is an ongoing conversation about the ethics and transparency surrounding shadow banning. The practice has been criticized for its lack of clarity, giving rise to advocacy for more transparent algorithms and appeal processes.

The Pros and Cons

While shadow banning is seen as a dark aspect of X, it's part of the platform's strategy to maintain a specific standard of content and user interaction. Understanding it isn't just about avoiding pitfalls but also about comprehending how the X ecosystem self-regulates.

Conclusion

Navigating the shadowy waters of X's banning mechanisms might seem daunting, but knowledge is the first line of defense. Understanding what shadow banning is and how it operates enables you to create a more resilient strategy, thereby enhancing your prospects on this transformative social media platform. In the next chapter, we will delve into the synergies between X and the crypto-world, and how they can be leveraged for greater financial gains.

NETWORKING IN THE AGE OF X

In the intricate ecosystem of X, relationships are the golden threads that connect individuals, ideas, and opportunities. As the platform evolves, so too does the art of networking. This chapter explores how X has transformed networking from a simple 'follow-for-follow' model to a multi-dimensional, algorithmically-enhanced interaction matrix that can significantly impact your financial gains and industry influence.

The Basics of Networking on X

On the surface, networking on X may appear similar to other social media platforms: you follow people, get followed back, and interact through likes, retweets, and comments. But what sets X apart is the weightage given to these interactions by its algorithm, which directly impacts your revenue generation capabilities.

Quality Over Quantity

X's algorithmic model puts a premium on meaningful interaction. It's no longer just about having the most followers; it's about having the right followers and engaging with them in a way that adds value. The more meaningful your interactions, the higher your impression rate, and thus, your earning potential.

Targeted Networking Strategies

Curate Your Circle: Choose who you follow wisely, considering factors like industry, interests, and the kind of value they could bring to your network.

Leverage Lists: X allows you to categorize your connections into lists, making it easier to share targeted content and measure its impact.

Engage with Influencers: A retweet or reply from an industry influencer can dramatically increase your impressions and, by extension, your revenue.

Symbiotic Relationships

X has created an environment where networking can lead to mutually beneficial relationships. For instance, content creators often enter revenue-sharing agreements, promoting each other's content to maximize impression rates collectively.

Real-Time Networking through Trends

One of the unique features of X is its real-time trending topics. Engaging with these trends can skyrocket your visibility, but it has to be done carefully to avoid penalties like shadow banning.

Avoiding Networking Pitfalls

Don't Spam: Sending mass messages or indiscriminately tagging people can have negative repercussions.

Be Authentic: People can spot inauthentic behavior from a mile away, and it's a sure-fire way to get unfollowed or even reported.

Privacy Boundaries: Don't invade others' privacy by unsolicited DMs or by sharing their content without permission.

Case Studies

We'll take a look at some real-world examples of individuals who have leveraged X's networking capabilities to expand their brand and skyrocket their earnings.

Future of Networking on X

As X continues to evolve, so will its networking capabilities. With the integration of AI tools for predictive networking and the growing importance of virtual communities in the Metaverse, the future of networking on X holds limitless potential.

Conclusion

Networking on X is a dynamic, ever-evolving art form. By understanding the algorithmic incentives and potential pitfalls, you can significantly optimize your networking strategy. As we move forward into an increasingly interconnected digital era, your network could very well become your most valuable asset. In the next chapter, we will explore how X interfaces with the world of cryptocurrencies, unlocking further avenues for wealth generation.

ANALYTICS UNVEILED: MAKING DATA YOUR ALLY

In an age where data reigns supreme, understanding and utilizing analytics can make the difference between a thriving online presence and an unnoticed one. X, with its sophisticated algorithm and revenue model, offers a rich set of analytics tools that can be the key to unlocking your digital potential. This chapter will demystify the art of data interpretation, providing actionable strategies to improve your visibility and, ultimately, your earnings on X.

The Importance of Analytics

Analytics serve as the compass in your X journey, providing invaluable insights into what's working and what isn't. By analyzing metrics like impressions, engagement rates, follower demographics, and more, you can tailor your content to reach and impact the right audience.

Getting Started with X Analytics

This section will walk you through the basics of setting up and accessing your analytics dashboard on X. You'll learn about key metrics, what they mean, and how to set up custom tracking for specialized campaigns.

Metrics to Keep an Eye On

Impressions: The cornerstone of X's revenue model, the more impressions your posts get, the higher your earnings.

Engagement Rate: These measures how many interactions (likes, retweets, replies) your posts get in relation to the number of impressions.

Click-Through Rate: Especially important for links and multimedia content, this tells you how effective your content is at encouraging further action.

Follower Demographics: Understanding who follows you can help you tailor your content to maximize impressions and engagement.

A/B Testing: The Trial and Error Method

One of the most effective ways to understand what works is by using A/B testing. This involves posting two or more variants of content to see which performs better. Here you'll learn how to set up A/B tests and how to interpret the results.

Understanding Shadow Banning in Analytics

A sudden, unexplained drop in your analytics could be a sign of shadow banning. Understanding how to read this through your analytics and what corrective measures to take is crucial for sustained growth.

Case Studies: Using Analytics for Success

This section will highlight real-world examples of X users who used analytics to transform their strategies and see exponential growth in both followers and revenue.

Advanced Analytics: Beyond the Basics

For those ready to dive deeper, this part will introduce more advanced analytics tools that integrate with X, offering even more nuanced insights. These could include heat maps of engagement, AI-driven content suggestions, and predictive analytics.

Conclusion: Turning Data into Algorithmic Gold

As the saying goes, "What gets measured gets managed." By making analytics your ally, you not only gain a deeper understanding of your existing network but also unlock insights that can help you strategically expand it. This crucial skill set will serve you well as you continue to navigate the ever-evolving landscape of X and the digital world at large.

In the next chapter, we will take a leap from analytics to cryptocurrencies, dissecting how digital assets like Ethereum, XRP, and Dogecoin are outpacing Bitcoin in the race for financial supremacy.

THE CRYPTOCURRENCY CONUNDRUM

The digital revolution is not limited to social media platforms like X; it also extends to the financial world, radically transforming how we perceive and handle money. Cryptocurrency, a decentralized form of digital or virtual currency, has become a household name, and certain coins are making a more significant impact than others. This chapter will delve into why Ethereum, XRP, and Dogecoin are considered more advantageous than Bitcoin, and how they intersect with X's ecosystem.

The Rise of Cryptocurrency

A brief overview of the history and meteoric rise of cryptocurrency, explaining the foundational technology of blockchain and how decentralized finance (DeFi) is reshaping traditional financial systems.

Ethereum: The Smart Contract Pioneer

Understanding Ethereum, its smart contract functionality, and why it's poised to be a game-changer in the world of digital transactions and beyond. We'll also look at how Ethereum integrates with X's payment and advertising systems.

XRP: The Digital Payment Protocol

Detailing what sets XRP apart from its competitors, primarily its focus on facilitating real-time, cross-border payments, and how XRP can potentially play a role in the X ecosystem for quicker and more efficient transactions.

Dogecoin: The Meme Coin with Real Value

Unpacking the journey of Dogecoin from a humorous meme to a significant player in the crypto world. How does its light-hearted origin and community involvement make it different, and could it be used in novel ways within X?

Bitcoin: The First but Not the Fittest

Understanding the limitations of Bitcoin in terms of scalability, environmental concerns, and transaction speed, providing a context for why Ethereum, XRP, and Dogecoin offer more sustainable and efficient alternatives.

Cryptocurrency and X: A Profitable Partnership

Exploring the symbiotic relationship between X and cryptocurrencies, how the two can work together to provide a seamless, efficient, and profitable user experience.

Investing in Crypto: Risks and Rewards

Cryptocurrency is volatile, and while there are enormous gains to be had, there are also significant risks. This section provides strategies for risk mitigation while investing in crypto, along with case studies of how these strategies have worked for some X influencers.

Future Outlook: NFTs, DeFi, and Beyond

A look into how Non-Fungible Tokens (NFTs), DeFi projects, and other blockchain-based innovations could further intertwine with X and offer exciting new avenues for income and engagement.

Conclusion: The Financial Landscape Reimagined

The advent of cryptocurrencies like Ethereum, XRP, and Dogecoin, alongside platforms like X, represents a transformative moment in both social engagement and financial empowerment. Understanding these shifts will prepare you for a future where digital assets and online platforms will increasingly become integrated parts of our daily lives.

In the following chapter, we'll explore the role artificial intelligence plays in this brave new digital world, focusing on its potential to both disrupt and create new career paths.

NFTS: YOUR DIGITAL SIGNATURE

The rise of Non-Fungible Tokens (NFTs) has captivated the imagination of artists, collectors, and the broader public. With NFTs representing unique digital assets verified using blockchain technology, they hold significant promise in various fields beyond art, including digital identity, real estate, and more. In this chapter, we explore how NFTs work, their synergy with X, and why they may be the next big thing in personal branding and income generation.

What Are NFTs?

A beginner-friendly introduction explaining the concept of NFTs, their uniqueness compared to fungible tokens like cryptocurrencies, and the technological foundation that enables this uniqueness.

The NFT Ecosystem

An overview of the various platforms and marketplaces that allow the creation, buying, selling, and trading of NFTs. This section also discusses how different types of NFTs—art, collectibles, virtual real estate—offer different forms of value.

NFTs and Personal Branding

How NFTs are increasingly used to represent a form of digital signature or brand identity. With the ability to attach your name to unique digital assets, creators can differentiate themselves in crowded spaces, particularly within X's environment.

NFTs on X: The Ideal Partnership?

A closer look at how X, with its revenue models and wide-reaching audience, provides fertile ground for the popularization and utilization of NFTs. Discussions could include theoretical features where X integrates NFTs into its platform to authenticate unique posts, artwork, or even moments.

Monetizing Content: NFTs as Residual Income

Exploring the ways NFTs can serve as a long-term revenue model for artists and creators. Understand how ownership and royalties can be built into NFTs, enabling creators to earn as their work gains popularity.

Risks and Ethical Considerations

Though they hold tremendous promise, NFTs aren't without their drawbacks. This section will discuss the ethical and environmental concerns associated with NFTs, such as their carbon footprint and potential for copyright infringement.

NFTs in the Mainstream

As major companies and celebrities begin to engage with NFTs, we examine what mainstream acceptance means for individual creators and investors, particularly those who are active on X.

Future Prospects: NFTs and the Metaverse

How can NFTs evolve from here? We look at the future of NFTs, particularly in virtual worlds, digital real estate, and other blockchain-powered ecosystems, considering how these developments might integrate with X or compete with it.

Conclusion: Your Asset, Your Legacy

NFTs offer a ground-breaking way for creators to have control over their digital assets and their brand. As X continues to develop, the symbiosis between NFTs and X is likely to grow stronger, creating new opportunities for creators and investors alike.

In the next chapter, we will delve into the revolutionary world of artificial intelligence, examining its potential to both disrupt existing industries and create entirely new ones.

THE RISE OF DEFI: DECENTRALIZED FINANCE EXPLAINED

Decentralized Finance, commonly known as DeFi, is a revolutionary development that aims to democratize access to financial services. It accomplishes this by using blockchain technology to create decentralized protocols and platforms that can perform the same functions as traditional banks but without intermediaries. This chapter delves into the dynamics of DeFi, its relevance in today's digital landscape, and its implications for users of X social media.

What is DeFi?

An introduction to the core principles behind Decentralized Finance. This section demystifies the term and elaborates on its key components, including lending platforms, decentralized exchanges, stable coins, and yield farming.

The Architecture of DeFi

Understanding the fundamental technologies that make DeFi possible: blockchain, smart contracts, decentralized applications (dApps), and more. Here, we'll explain how these elements come together to create a secure, transparent, and equitable financial ecosystem.

How DeFi Intersects with X

Examining how X social media users can benefit from DeFi applications. The features like P2P payments, crowd-funding campaigns, and even decentralized content monetization models that could potentially integrate with X are discussed in detail.

Decentralized Exchanges: Beyond Traditional Trading

An exploration of decentralized exchanges (DEXs) which allow users to trade cryptocurrencies and other assets without relying on centralized entities. Understand how these platforms offer increased privacy, control, and often lower fees.

Yield Farming and Liquidity Pools

An essential guide to yield farming strategies and liquidity pools, showcasing how users can earn returns by providing liquidity or participating in a DeFi protocol. This section provides practical tips for X users who are interested in getting into yield farming.

Risks and Concerns

While DeFi offers immense benefits, it also comes with its own set of risks. This section highlights potential pitfalls such as smart contract vulnerabilities, impermanent loss, and regulatory uncertainty. Here we will also address the need for due diligence and proper risk assessment.

DeFi in the Spotlight: Case Studies

Real-world examples of DeFi projects that have made a significant impact. This will include case studies of projects that have either integrated with X or have the potential to do so.

The Regulatory Landscape

As DeFi grows, so does the attention it receives from regulatory bodies. An overview of existing and potential regulations affecting DeFi and what this means for the average X user.

The Future of DeFi and X

Looking forward at how the symbiosis between DeFi and X could evolve. Will DeFi protocols become a standard feature on X, or will they develop separately but remain complementary?

Conclusion: Financial Freedom in the Palm of Your Hand

Decentralized finance offers pathways to financial empowerment and independence. As the world continues to evolve digitally, the amalgamation of DeFi and social platforms like X is likely to become more profound, opening up new avenues for wealth creation and financial security.

A NEW ERA OF ADVERTISING

In the age of X social media and algorithmic monetization, advertising has undergone a significant metamorphosis. No longer confined to the traditional realms of print, television, and digital banners, the advertising industry has embraced new, sophisticated ways of reaching and engaging audiences. This chapter offers a comprehensive view of this new era of advertising, examining how it is deeply intertwined with X and other emerging technologies like Artificial Intelligence and blockchain.

From Banners to Algorithms

This section traces the evolution of advertising from its traditional forms to its current state, which is increasingly reliant on complex algorithms for targeting and engagement. We'll discuss how machine learning and data science have transformed advertising from a shotgun approach to a laser-focused strategy.

Sponsored Content on X: A Win-Win Scenario

X's unique revenue model allows for new kinds of sponsored content that are beneficial for both the platform and its users. This section will explain how X has monetized sponsored content and the kinds of opportunities this has created for advertisers and content creators alike.

The Role of AI and Machine Learning

Artificial Intelligence is not just changing the way we interact with platforms but also how advertisers interact with us. AI enables real-time data analysis, predictive analytics, and personalized content delivery, revolutionizing the advertising models on X.

Transparency and User Control

One of the key advantages of the new advertising paradigms is the increased level of transparency and control for the user. This section explores how blockchain could further these principles, making advertising more equitable and less intrusive.

Tokenization and Crypto Rewards

Understanding the rise of token-based rewards systems for user engagement and advertising. This would explain how some platforms are offering crypto tokens as rewards for watching ads or engaging with sponsored content, and how this might integrate with X in the future.

Localized and Community-Driven Ads

A look at how advertising can be more localized and community-driven on platforms like X, particularly with the use of decentralized technology and smart contracts.

Advertising in the Metaverse

As digital realities become increasingly integral to our lives, advertising is set to transcend into virtual worlds and augmented experiences. This section offers an imaginative look at what advertising might look like in the Metaverse and how X could play a role in this new frontier.

Regulatory Concerns and Ethical Considerations

The digital advertising landscape is not without its challenges, including concerns about data privacy, regulation, and ethical implications. This section tackles these issues head-on, offering insights into how they can be mitigated.

The Future is Personalized

The chapter concludes by speculating on the future of advertising in the era of X and beyond. Personalized, real-time, less intrusive yet more effective, the future of advertising looks promising for all parties involved—consumers, advertisers, and platforms.

Up next, we'll delve into how X is affecting social dynamics and relationships, both online and offline, in a world increasingly mediated by algorithms and digital interfaces.

AI AND CONTENT CREATION

The surge in Artificial Intelligence and machine learning technologies is causing ripples across various industries, and content creation is no exception. This chapter aims to explore how AI is transforming the landscape of content creation, focusing particularly on its impact within the X social media ecosystem.

AI-Generated Content: A New Frontier

We start with an introduction to AI-generated content, exploring tools and platforms that allow for automated text, image, and video creation. The pros and cons of AI-generated content will be discussed, as well as its current and potential future role in X.

Writing Assistants and Ghost-Writing 2.0

This section delves into the role of AI writing assistants like OpenAI's GPT-4 and how they are revolutionizing the ghost-writing industry. We explore how these tools can be harnessed for generating engaging and relevant content on X, aiding in monetization efforts.

Machine Learning and Analytics

Understanding your audience is critical for effective content creation. This segment looks at how machine learning algorithms analyse data and provide insights that can guide creators in crafting content that resonates with their audience on X.

Content Personalization and Curation

Here, we investigate how AI is helping in content personalization and curation. The algorithms behind X's content feed are a complex tapestry of machine learning models that aim to deliver a personalized user experience. How can content creators use this to their advantage?

Visual Media: AI in Image and Video Editing

Visual content is a crucial part of digital communication. This section explores how AI can assist in image and video editing, making the process faster, easier, and more sophisticated. This is especially relevant for creators looking to diversify their content offerings on X.

Ethical Considerations and Bias

AI is not without its ethical dilemmas. This section delves into concerns around data privacy, content originality, and algorithmic bias. How do these ethical considerations affect AI's role in content creation on X?

Real-world Case Studies

We'll take a look at some real-world case studies of influencers, marketers, and other content creators who have successfully leveraged AI technologies to enhance their presence and profitability on X.

Future Trends: AI and Metaverse

As we peer into the future, we consider how AI will interact with other emergent technologies like the Metaverse. Could AI-generated avatars be the next big influencers on X? What role will AI play in content creation within virtual worlds?

Conclusion: Navigating the AI-Enabled Future

We wrap up this chapter by providing some actionable insights and recommendations for content creators looking to successfully navigate the AI-enabled future on X. From leveraging AI tools for content creation to understanding the ethical landscape, the goal is to equip you with the knowledge you need to stay ahead of the curve.

In the next chapter, we'll explore another transformative technology that is making its mark on the digital landscape: virtual and augmented reality. Stay tuned as we delve into how these technologies are reshaping the way we interact with digital content and each other.

THE FUTURE OF JOURNALISM IN THE X AGE

In a world increasingly dominated by social media platforms like X, the traditional landscape of journalism faces existential questions. This chapter seeks to explore the intersection of journalism and X's unique ecosystem, examining both the challenges and opportunities that lie ahead.

Decentralization of News Distribution

The first section takes a look at how X has decentralized the news distribution model, empowering individual journalists, influencers, and even everyday users to break news stories. What does this mean for established media houses and freelance journalists?

Verification in the Age of Fake News

As news generation becomes increasingly democratized, the need for accurate verification methods becomes critical. This section explores the tools and technologies, including blockchain and AI, that can be used for fact-checking and validation within the X ecosystem.

Citizen Journalism: A Double-Edged Sword

The rise of citizen journalism has its merits and pitfalls. We explore how X enables real-time, on-the-ground reporting but also poses challenges like misinformation and lack of journalistic ethics. Real-world examples and case studies will be discussed.

Monetization Strategies for Journalists

Understanding how to monetize journalistic content on X can be a game-changer. This section offers strategies and examples of how journalists can use the platform's algorithmic revenue model to their advantage, from subscriptions to sponsored content.

Reporting in 280 Characters: The Art of Brevity

For those journalists who don't have a subscription to X, the challenge of reporting news in a constrained format remains. This section explores how to make each word count, providing tips and strategies for impactful reporting within 280 characters.

Data-Driven Journalism: Making Use of Analytics

In the era of big data, understanding analytics can offer a competitive edge. This section will examine how journalists can use analytics to understand readership patterns, trending topics, and even predict future news trends.

Long-Form Journalism in the X Age

Despite the brevity-focused nature of social media, long-form journalism still has a place. This segment delves into how feature stories and investigative reports can be effectively distributed and monetized through X.

Collaboration and Networking

Journalists have always relied on networks for tips and stories, but X takes it to a new level. We explore how to network effectively within the X community, making use of the platform's unique features for collaborative reporting.

Legal and Ethical Considerations

What are the legal ramifications of reporting on X? This section will discuss issues like copyright, defamation, and data protection, providing guidelines for ethical journalism in the digital age.

Conclusion: Charting a Sustainable Path

The chapter concludes by looking ahead to the future of journalism in the age of X and other digital platforms. From adopting new technologies to understanding the evolving landscape, journalists will need to be agile and adaptable to succeed in this new paradigm.

CAREERS OF THE FUTURE: WHAT AI CAN'T REPLACE

As Artificial Intelligence continues to disrupt traditional industries, the question of what careers will endure becomes increasingly relevant. This chapter delves into the professional paths that are not only resistant to automation but may thrive in an AI-driven world.

Emotional Intelligence: The Human Touch

The first section highlights the importance of emotional intelligence in careers like counseling, social work, and healthcare. Despite technological advancements, AI can't replicate the empathy, understanding, and nuanced communication required in these fields.

Creative Professions: The Art of Originality

While AI can generate art, write music, and even craft stories, the creative impulse behind true innovation remains a distinctly human trait. This section explores why careers in arts, design, and other creative fields will continue to value human ingenuity.

Strategic Thinking and Complex Problem-Solving

AI excels at tasks with defined parameters but struggles with open-ended problems that require a nuanced understanding of context. Professions like strategic consultancy, public policy analysis, and high-level management rely on these skills and will continue to do so.

Education and Lifelong Learning

While e-learning platforms and AI tutors are on the rise, the role of teachers, mentors, and educators remains irreplaceable. This section discusses the evolving nature of education and how human educators can integrate AI tools to create a more enriching learning experience.

Craftsmanship: The Value of Skilled Labour

From carpentry to gourmet cooking, certain crafts require a level of skill, expertise, and attention to detail that AI can't replicate. This section honours the value of craftsmanship and explores how these careers will endure in the digital age.

The Role of Ethics: Moral Considerations in AI

AI's limitations extend to the realm of ethics and moral reasoning. Professions that require ethical considerations, like bioethics, legal work, and even journalism, will continue to need human involvement for balanced and morally sound decisions.

Research and Scientific Exploration

The quest for knowledge and the spirit of exploration are fundamentally human endeavours. This section discusses how roles in research and science will continue to be driven by human curiosity, ingenuity, and the willingness to venture into the unknown.

Social and Community Roles

From activists to community organizers, careers cantered around social change and community building require a depth of human connection and understanding that AI cannot provide. This section discusses the enduring importance of these roles.

Conclusion: The Harmonious Coexistence of Man and Machine

The chapter concludes by exploring how AI can act as a tool to augment human capabilities rather than replace them. It suggests a future where humans and AI work in tandem, each augmenting the other's strengths and compensating for weaknesses.

SUCCESS STORIES: X BILLIONAIRES

The meteoric rise of X as a social media platform has given birth to a new class of digital billionaires. This chapter dives into the stories of these successful individuals, showcasing how they harnessed the power of X, cryptocurrency, and AI to generate staggering amounts of wealth.

The Influencer Turned Mogul

This section covers the journey of an influencer who capitalized on X's algorithmic revenue model and subscription offerings to build an empire. It delves into their strategic partnerships, branding moves, and how they successfully transitioned from a content creator to a business magnate.

The Meme Lord

The world of memes isn't just for laughs anymore; it's big business. This section follows a meme creator who has turned viral content into a revenue-generating machine. With an impressive following and clever monetization strategies, this individual became an X billionaire almost overnight.

The Artist and the NFT Goldmine

With the rise of NFTs, artists now have a ground-breaking way to monetize their work. This part explores the journey of an artist who went from obscurity to becoming a multi-millionaire, all thanks to their savvy use of X and NFT platforms.

The Video Visionary

As X introduced video monetization, a new wave of content creators entered the platform. This section follows a visionary who utilized the video medium to capture a massive audience, ultimately raking in millions through ad revenue, sponsorships, and merchandising.

The Crypto Evangelist

Cryptocurrency has offered an entirely new way to invest and grow wealth. This segment tells the story of an early adopter and evangelist who leveraged X to educate the masses about Ethereum, XRP, and Dogecoin, subsequently amassing a fortune in the process.

The AI Pioneer

Artificial Intelligence is transforming our world, and those at the forefront stand to gain immensely. This part discusses an individual who used AI-powered tools to enhance their X content, resulting in exponential growth and, eventually, billionaire status.

The Community Builder

Some have used X as a platform for social change and community-building. This section covers the story of an individual who capitalized on this aspect to generate wealth by bringing people together around causes, events, or shared interests.

The Underdog: From Zero to Billionaire

The chapter concludes with an inspiring story of an underdog who started with no following, no influence, but a whole lot of determination. Through hard work, strategic networking, and leveraging X's unique features, they defied the odds to become a billionaire.

By studying these success stories, you'll gain valuable insights into what it takes to thrive in the new digital landscape dominated by X, cryptocurrency, and AI. As we transition into the next chapter, we'll discuss strategies and actionable tips to help you become the next X success story. Stay tuned.

PITFALLS TO AVOID

Navigating the complex and ever-changing landscape of X and the digital world comes with its share of challenges. This chapter outlines common mistakes, oversights, and pitfalls that you should be aware of as you set out on your journey to algorithmic gold.

Over-Reliance on Algorithms

While algorithms can boost your reach and revenue, an over-reliance on them can be perilous. The algorithms can change at any time, affecting your visibility and engagement rates. Diversify your content and keep your audience engaged through authentic interactions.

Ignoring the Shadow Ban

The shadow ban is a real concern for X users looking to maximize their revenue. Being shadow banned can severely limit your content's reach, thereby affecting your income. Understanding how to navigate this is crucial for long-term success.

Bot Backfires

In an attempt to gain quick popularity, some users resort to bots for likes and follows. This section discusses the downsides of using such shortcuts, including potential suspension from X and tarnished credibility.

Bad Crypto Investments

Not every cryptocurrency will make you a billionaire. Investing without research or understanding market trends can lead to significant financial loss. Be wary of 'pump and dump' schemes and keep an eye on regulatory developments.

Overlooking Security

The digital world is fraught with security risks, from account hacking to identity theft. Ensuring the security of your X account and cryptocurrency wallets is imperative for your financial well-being.

Plagiarism and Copyright Issues

The temptation to repost popular content can be strong, especially when you see others gaining massive amounts of impressions from it. However, plagiarism and copyright infringement can lead to legal consequences and reputational damage.

Misunderstanding DeFi and NFTs

Decentralized Finance (DeFi) and NFTs offer lucrative opportunities but come with their own sets of risks. Being uninformed can result in bad investments, financial losses, and missed opportunities.

Neglecting Community and Networking

Engagement isn't just about posting content. Ignoring the social aspect of social media, such as community-building and networking, can lead to a stagnant follower count and limited reach.

Underestimating AI's Limitations

While AI can help automate many tasks, it's not a complete substitute for human creativity and strategy. Knowing when to leverage AI—and when not to—is essential for long-term success.

By avoiding these common pitfalls, you can better equip yourself for the challenges and opportunities that lie ahead in the world of X, cryptocurrency, and artificial intelligence. The next chapter will provide actionable tips and strategies to set you on the path to becoming a digital billionaire.

BUILDING A BRAND ON X

In a world where digital presence can make or break a business, building a strong brand on X has never been more critical. Unlike other social media platforms, X has carved a unique path that allows for more than just user engagement; it enables revenue generation directly from the platform. With its rebranding and new features, understanding how to navigate this territory is crucial. Here, we will dive into how you can use X to build a powerful brand that resonates with your target audience and, ultimately, brings in "algorithmic gold."

The Importance of Branding on X

Branding isn't just about a logo or a catchy tagline anymore. It's a multifaceted approach that encompasses everything you do, from your content to your engagement with your audience. On X, your brand is your identity. With the platform's various monetization strategies, having a cohesive brand can directly influence your revenue stream.

Know Your Audience

Before you start posting, understand who you're trying to reach. Utilize X's robust analytics to see who's engaging with your content. Are they the audience you're targeting? If not, it's time to rethink your strategy.

Quality Over Quantity

X is not a platform where you can mindlessly churn out content. Given its algorithmic revenue model, the quality of your posts directly impacts your earnings. Invest time in creating high-value content that not only engages but also enriches your audience.

Leveraging Features for Branding

With the subscription model, longer Tweets, and video monetization, X provides unique features you can't find on other platforms. Use them wisely. For instance, longer posts allow you to delve deeper into topics, providing valuable insights that 280 characters could never achieve.

Consistency is Key

Once you've found your voice, stay consistent. Consistency in tone, content type, and posting schedule can significantly boost your brand recognition. If people like what they see, they'll keep coming back for more.

Engaging with the Community

Remember, X is a social platform first. Don't underestimate the power of community. Engage with your followers, participate in relevant conversations, and don't shy away from collaborations. Interactivity boosts your brand's visibility, contributing to higher impressions and, consequently, greater revenue.

Analytics: Your Brand's Best Friend

Finally, always keep an eye on analytics. The numbers never lie and can offer invaluable insights into what's working and what's not. Use these statistics to refine your approach continually.

Conclusion

Building a brand on X is not just beneficial; it's essential for anyone looking to maximize their earning potential on the platform. It's a multifaceted endeavour that requires a deep understanding of the platform's unique features, a keen eye for analytics, and an unyielding commitment to quality and consistency. So go ahead, start building your brand on X, and watch as the algorithmic gold starts to flow into your account.

LOCAL IMPACT, GLOBAL REACH

The beauty of X as a social media platform lies not just in its innovative revenue models or its algorithmic prowess but also in its ability to transcend geographical borders. By cleverly leveraging the features and functionalities of X, brands, influencers, and ordinary users alike can make a significant local impact while also reaching a global audience. In this chapter, we explore the strategies and tactics that can help you achieve this duality, creating ripple effects that begin in your community and radiate outwards.

The Localization of Content

Creating content that resonates with your local audience should be the first step. Tailoring your posts to local trends, culture, and dialects can provide a much-needed initial boost. However, always keep a global perspective in mind. The nuanced art of balancing both local and international elements in your content can be a strong differentiator. X's analytics can help you understand which local elements have global appeal.

Leveraging Local Networks

On X, networking doesn't have to start at a global scale. By engaging with local businesses, artists, and thought leaders, you can create a support system that encourages shared growth. X's recommendation algorithms often favor well-connected accounts, so a robust local network can provide a launching pad for international exposure.

Participate in Global Conversations

While keeping your roots in local soil, don't hesitate to jump into global conversations that align with your brand and personal interests. Whether it's a social cause, an international event, or a trending topic, participating in global discussions increases your visibility far beyond your geographical boundaries.

Translate and Adapt

Language can be a barrier, but it can also be an opportunity. If you notice that a significant part of your audience comes from non-English-speaking countries, consider creating content in multiple languages. X's extended character limits for premium accounts make it easier to express complex ideas in more than one language.

Analytics: The Guide to Scaling

Scaling from local to global requires a keen understanding of analytics. X provides detailed insights that can tell you where your audience is based, what content they engage with the most, and when they are most active. This data is invaluable in adapting your local strategies for a global stage.

The Power of Collaboration

One of the fastest ways to extend your local impact to a global scale is through strategic collaborations. Partner with individuals or brands that align with your values but are based in different regions. This mutual relationship can expose each of you to the other's audience, creating a win-win situation.

Sustainability and Responsibility

As you grow from a local influencer to a global phenomenon on X, the responsibility you carry also scales. A wrong word or misguided post can have consequences that are as significant globally as they are locally. Always be conscious of the sustainability and ethical implications of what you're putting out into the world.

Conclusion

In the age of X, the dichotomy between local and global is fading fast. The platform empowers each one of its users to be a global citizen, albeit with strong local roots. Mastering the art of balancing the two can be your pathway to unprecedented success on this ground-breaking social media platform. Make a local impact, but always keep your eyes on the global horizon.

THE ETHICAL CONSIDERATIONS OF X

As with any technological innovation, the rise of X as a dominant social media platform brings with it a range of ethical considerations that users, influencers, and even the company itself must grapple with. In this chapter, we delve into the moral and ethical dilemmas that are inherent in X's ecosystem, offering guidance for responsible engagement.

Data Privacy and User Consent

The cornerstone of any digital platform is data. X is no exception, with its algorithmic revenue model heavily reliant on user data to drive impressions and engagement. However, this raises the question: how much of this data collection is consensual and transparent? It's essential for users to familiarize themselves with X's privacy policies and settings, and for X to continue to uphold stringent privacy standards.

The Bot Dilemma

Elon Musk's approach to combating the "vast armies of bots" involves a paywall, making it cost-ineffective for bot creators to flood the platform. While this approach may seem practical, it also raises ethical concerns. By introducing a financial barrier to entry, are we sacrificing the egalitarian spirit of social media? And what about bots that serve useful, or even crucial, functions?

Mental Health and Revenue Motivation

The new revenue models incentivize user engagement to an unprecedented extent, encouraging content creators to prioritize virality and impressions. However, this creates an atmosphere of constant competition, potentially leading to burnout and affecting mental health. Where do we draw the line between financial incentives and the well-being of the users?

Ethical Advertising

With X's algorithmic power steering its advertising model, ethical considerations in the kind of ads displayed become increasingly significant. Is the platform promoting products or services that could be harmful, divisive, or prey on vulnerable individuals? Both advertisers and the platform must ensure that ethical standards are maintained.

Content Moderation and Free Speech

The issue of content moderation is a delicate balancing act. On the one hand, X needs to ensure that harmful or misleading content is filtered out. On the other, there's a fine line between moderation and censorship. How does X ensure it doesn't stifle free speech while maintaining a safe environment for its users?

Environmental Impact

The energy footprint of running massive data centres for X's operations is often overlooked. As discussions around climate change gain momentum, it becomes crucial for X to adopt sustainable practices and for users to demand such responsibility from the platform.

Social Responsibility

As a major player influencing public opinion and behaviors, X carries a significant social responsibility. It's not just about what's allowed on the platform; it's also about what is endorsed. X needs to be cautious about the kind of content and conversations it promotes, ensuring they align with ethical standards and social well-being.

Conclusion

The ethical considerations surrounding X are vast and multi-faceted, requiring constant evaluation and adjustment from both the platform and its users. While the opportunities for financial gain and global reach are enticing, they must be balanced against the ethical implications of our actions in this digital realm. Only with thoughtful and responsible engagement can we hope to make the most of what X has to offer, without sacrificing our ethical principles.

THE EVOLUTION OF X

As we close the curtains on this expansive exploration into the world of X, it is only fitting to look ahead at what the future holds for this ground-breaking platform. Much like any technology, X is not static; it is a dynamic entity, continually evolving in response to user needs, market forces, and advances in technology. In this final chapter, we'll discuss several trajectories that could shape the next era of X.

Technological Innovations

While X has already incorporated a number of state-of-the-art features—ranging from AI-powered analytics to intricate algorithmic revenue models—the ceaseless march of technological innovation promises even more transformative changes. Could we see the incorporation of virtual reality (VR) into the platform, allowing for a more immersive social media experience? Will quantum computing play a role in delivering even more sophisticated algorithms? The possibilities are endless.

Expanding the Subscription Model

X's Premium subscription model has proven to be successful in both generating revenue and enhancing user engagement. As the platform matures, we could see the introduction of tiered subscription models, each offering different levels of customization, analytics, and monetization options to cater to various user needs.

Regulatory Changes

As social media platforms like X gain power and influence, they increasingly come under the scrutiny of governments worldwide. New data protection laws, antitrust regulations, and content moderation requirements could dramatically affect how X operates. This is a space that requires close watching for anyone invested in the platform, either as a content creator or as a consumer.

User-Generated Evolution

One of the most exciting aspects of X is its responsiveness to user behavior. The platform has shown a willingness to adapt and change based on how people engage with its features. This opens the door to a future shaped collaboratively by the platform and its user base. User feedback could lead to features that we have not yet even conceived.

Convergence with Other Technologies

The interconnected digital landscape means that X doesn't exist in a vacuum. As seen in previous chapters, its success is closely tied to advancements in related fields like cryptocurrency, AI, and even decentralized finance (DeFi). As these technologies evolve, so too will X, potentially in ways that redefine social media's role in our lives.

The Role of AI and Automation

Artificial Intelligence will continue to play an increasingly critical role in the functioning of X. From enhanced content discovery to more nuanced audience targeting for advertisements, the influence of AI on X's ecosystem will only grow over time. Additionally, automation tools might take over mundane tasks, allowing users to focus more on content creation and engagement.

Global Expansion

Thus far, X's reach has been impressive, but it's far from a truly global platform. Market-specific features and localization efforts could open up new geographies, each with its unique opportunities and challenges.

Conclusion

The story of X is far from over. Like any evolving entity, it will face challenges and opportunities in equal measure. But what remains unchanged is its transformative power—a power that extends beyond simple social interactions to influence economics, politics, culture, and more. As we look ahead, it's clear that X will continue to be a key player in shaping the digital landscape, offering new avenues for wealth creation, social engagement, and even global change. Here's to the future—a future that promises to be as exciting as it is unpredictable.

THE FINAL STRATEGY: YOUR ROADMAP TO X BILLIONAIRE STATUS

As we culminate this comprehensive journey through the world of X, it's time to distil everything you've learned into a concrete strategy. While becoming a billionaire on X—or any platform—is not guaranteed, understanding the dynamics of this evolving digital frontier can significantly enhance your odds of success. Here is your final roadmap, designed to provide you with the tactical steps and strategic thinking required to make your mark on this revolutionary platform.

Understand the Algorithm

By now, you know that the algorithm is the engine that drives X. Before you jump in, spend time learning how your content is surfaced and promoted. Use analytics to gather data on user engagement and adapt your strategy accordingly. Treat the algorithm as your ally, not your adversary.

Choose the Right Subscription Model

The benefits of X's Premium subscription are manifold, from longer posts to advanced analytics. Weigh the costs and benefits and opt for the one that aligns with your needs and goals. Remember, investing in yourself is the first step toward monumental success.

Build an Authentic Brand

Your X profile is not just a social media account; it's a brand. From your profile picture to the type of content you post, every detail contributes to your public image. Be consistent, be genuine, and most importantly, be strategic.

Engage, Engage, Engage

No one achieves billionaire status by staying in their own bubble. Interact with other users, join trending conversations, and don't shy away from collaborations. Engagement is social currency; spend it wisely but generously.

Monetize Smartly

Don't just aim to go viral. Aim to monetize your viral moments. Whether it's through sponsored content, an e-commerce push, or funnelling followers to other revenue streams, always have a plan to convert fame into financial gain.

Optimize for Video Content

Video is the future of digital content. Learn how to create engaging, shareable videos that not only garner views but also drive action. From video ads to tutorials, the medium offers endless possibilities for those willing to invest in quality production.

Leverage Cryptocurrencies and NFTs

As discussed in earlier chapters, digital currencies and assets can amplify your earnings. Consider selling unique digital merchandise or tokens as a way to engage your fanbase, or use blockchain technologies to ensure transparent and frictionless transactions.

Avoid the Pitfalls

From shadow bans to ethical considerations, X is filled with potential hazards. Always remember to conduct yourself responsibly, both to uphold your brand and to avoid punitive actions from the platform.

Adapt and Evolve

The world of X will continue to change, and you'll need to change with it. Keep an eye on emerging trends, adapt to new features, and never stop learning. Your ability to evolve is your greatest asset.

Conclusion

Becoming a billionaire on X is a mammoth task, requiring a blend of creativity, business acumen, and a dash of luck. Yet, armed with the insights and strategies outlined in this book, you are now better equipped to tackle the challenges and seize the opportunities that lie ahead. So go forth and stake your claim on this digital frontier, where the only limit is the one you set for yourself. Welcome to the future. Welcome to X.

EPILOGUE: BEYOND THE HORIZON

As the digital ink dries on the pages of this book, it's essential to recognize that we are merely scratching the surface of a world in flux. The landscape of X and the broader digital universe is ever-changing— new features will be launched, algorithms will be tweaked, and innovative technologies will reshape the game.

While the title "Algorithmic Gold: The New Billionaires of X Social Media" suggests a focus on financial success, the book aims to serve a dual purpose. Beyond the monetization strategies and networking hacks, it's a guidebook for navigating a transformative era. The emergence of platforms like X heralds a time when individuals have unprecedented tools at their disposal—tools to share their voices, establish their brands, and influence global dialogues.

X is not merely a platform; it's an ecosystem. An ecosystem that grows more nuanced and complex with each passing day. The concepts discussed in the book—from subscription models to shadow banning, from cryptocurrencies to AI—are all part of this vibrant, dynamic environment.

So, what comes next? The horizon is ever-expanding. As blockchain technologies mature and AI becomes more sophisticated, we can only begin to imagine how these will integrate with platforms like X. Perhaps we will see new paradigms of trust, enabled by transparent, blockchain-based verification methods. Maybe AI will transform content creation to such an extent that human creators and AI collaborators work in seamless harmony. One thing is certain: change is the only constant.

It's your turn to seize this moment, to harness the full suite of tools and strategies outlined in these pages, and to set forth on your own journey toward not just financial success but meaningful impact. As you navigate the labyrinthine world of X, remember that this is more than just a game of algorithms and impressions—it's a revolutionary new way of connecting, sharing, and building something meaningful.

The final strategy, therefore, is not merely a list of tactical steps but an invitation: an invitation to engage, to innovate, and to lead in this exciting new era. Take your place at the forefront of this digital revolution. You are not just a player in this brave new world—you are also its architect.

Thank you for reading "Algorithmic Gold: The New Billionaires of X Social Media." Now, go create your future.

The end is just the beginning.

GLOSSARY

Algorithm

A set of rules and calculations that a computer follows to complete a task. In the context of X, the algorithm is used to determine content visibility, impressions, and potential revenue streams.

Analytics

The interpretation of data patterns to gain insights. In X, analytics can be used to understand user behavior, content performance, and the effectiveness of different strategies.

Blockchain

A decentralized and distributed digital ledger used to record transactions. It's the underlying technology for cryptocurrencies like Ethereum and XRP.

Blue Tick

A verification badge in social media platforms, including X, that indicates the authenticity of an account, often reserved for public figures, brands, and other high-profile accounts.

Content Monetization

The act of earning revenue through content creation, primarily through advertising, subscription models, or direct transactions.

Cryptocurrency

Digital or virtual currencies that use cryptography for security. Examples include Ethereum, XRP, and Dogecoin.

DeFi (Decentralized Finance)

A financial system built on blockchain technologies that is open to anyone and doesn't rely on intermediaries like banks.

Impressions

The total number of times a piece of content is displayed on someone's screen. Impressions are a key metric in X's revenue model.

NFT (Non-Fungible Token)

A type of digital asset that represents ownership of a unique item or piece of content, often used for digital art, collectibles, and other unique assets.

Premium Subscription

The paid tier on X that offers advanced features, such as an edit button, prioritized rankings, and longer posts.

Shadow Ban

An action taken by social media platforms, including X, where a user's content is suppressed or made less visible to others without notifying the user.

XRP

A digital payment protocol more than a cryptocurrency, XRP is used for representing the transfer of value across the XRP Ledger.

Rabbit Hole

In the context of X, a term used to describe a deep dive into interconnected topics, threads, or conversations that can lead to higher engagement levels.

Revenue Model

The strategy employed by a business to generate income. In the case of X, it includes impressions-based earnings, subscriptions, and monetized features.

Subscription Model

A business model where customers pay a recurring fee to gain access to a service or product, in this case, X's Premium tier.

Video Monetization

The process of generating income through the publication of video content. In the context of X, this refers to earning revenue through video impressions.

AI (Artificial Intelligence)

The simulation of human intelligence processes by machines, especially computer systems. AI tools like ghost-writing and Co-pilot can aid in content creation and other tasks.

Co-pilot

An AI-powered tool that assists in coding, providing suggestions and automating certain programming tasks.

Ghost-writing 2.0

A term used to describe the next level of automated writing services, often empowered by advanced AI.

AUTHOR'S LETTER

Dear Readers,

Thank you for taking the time to explore "Algorithmic Gold: The New Billionaires of X Social Media." The journey through the landscape of digital currencies, social media revolutions, and the untapped potential of technology has been a thrilling one, and I'm grateful to share it with all of you.

For Elon Musk and his X Team

Thank you for buying Twitter and converting it to X, giving us the opportunity to earn on our creativity. I want to gift you this message as a flower while you're still with us on Earth; keep doing the great job. I know it's hard now to figure out the programming, but the light will shine through one day, as long as you put humanity first. As someone who taught me about business once said, "First the people, and money will follow."

To All Creative People in the World

It doesn't matter how small or big your art, NFTs, DeFi, Blockchains, Music, memes, or pieces of writing are. Whether known or unknown, whether it rains or shines, no matter where you are in the world or what conditions you're facing—do it for the love. If you've lost everything, remember, you created those things once; you can create better ones again. Whether your computer was stolen, lost, or burned—it's your moment to shine. Show the world what you're made of. Consider this letter a jump start to reignite any lost dreams. I believe in you, no matter how impossible your dreams may sound. With X, show the world it's possible.

To the Rest of the People

Open-source was built collectively by people around the world—think of Linux, GitHub, and other projects. Unity in diversity is strength. Yes, there will be divisions because of differing views, but let those views build something better. Extend this unity into a community of people who think like you and share the same goals. Lastly, I love you all—arise and shine. Let's show the world what we're made of. X. We are Timeless.

Thoughts..............

Writing this book has been both a challenge and an opportunity, an exploration into the mechanics of our digital world. The landscape changes swiftly, and staying ahead requires constant learning and adaptation. I hope this book serves as a starting point, a catalyst for your own journeys into the realms of social media, digital currencies, and beyond.

Thank you for your time, your curiosity, and your willingness to engage with the ideas presented in this book. I look forward to seeing where this collective knowledge takes us.

Best wishes for the future. May your endeavours be ever successful and your dreams realized.

Sincerely,

Onesimus Malatji [THE BLENDER]

P.S. If you find value in this book, please share it with others who may benefit from it. The more we share, the more we grow, and the closer we come to realizing a truly interconnected global community.

~~~~~~~~~~~~~~~~~~~~END~~~~~~~~~~~~~~~~~~~~~